Eternal Searcher Song Book

by

Lee McQueen

McQueen♟Press

Published by McQueen Press
http://mcqueenpress.wordpress.com

"Black Diamond Crape Myrtle" cover image and design, interior design, typesetting by McQueen Press.

Author photo by McQueen Press.

"Black Queen" logo is a registered mark of McQueen Press and should not be copied without permission.

ISBN 978-1-7352369-8-8
Print version

"Choose, Tragedy's Dancer, Wild Hazy Beautiful Crazy, Yellow Rain (Gaslight), Aloof Truth, I Stand in Line, Phantasmic Fantastic Fantasy, Seven Months to Love You, Stuck on Maybe Not, First Time, God Gave This to Us, Universe, When My Man Plays, The Wind is an Eternal Searcher (Are You the Hero?)," previously published in *Things I Forgot to Tell You* [McQueen Press, 2007, 2nd ed]. Also registered as song lyrics with the Library of Congress by Lee McQueen, 2002.

"Amen" lyric ["Universe"], traditional gospel, public domain.

"Why I Versify," also published in *Things I Forgot to Tell You* [McQueenPress, 2007, 2nd ed].

"On Street K, Wild Hazy, Beautiful Crazy, Gaslight (Yellow Rain), Universe, Painted," also published in *Imaginarium* [McQueen Press, 2007]. Also registered with the Library of Congress.

"Wild Hazy, Beautiful Crazy" also published in *The Dark Fantastic* [McQueen Press, 2013] and *The Cadis Evening* [McQueen Press, 2016, 2nd ed 2020]. Also registered with the Library of Congress.

"Reverie" also published in *Road Romance: Tales from the Book Tour* [McQueen Press, 2013] and *Arusha: Poems & Essays* [McQueen Press, 2021]. Also registered with the Library of Congress.

"Silk and Silver" also published in *Sudan: The Lion of Truth*, 2nd ed [McQueen Press, 2011]. Also registered with the Library of Congress.

"Damaged: But We Still Love You, The Lion Roars, The People Live, The Sun Shines" also published in *Arusha: Poems & Essays* [McQueen Press, 2021]. Also registered with the Library of Congress.

Publisher's Catalog-in-Publication

McQueen, Lee, 1970-
Eternal Searcher Song Book/Lee McQueen
    1. Poems
    2. Song lyrics
    3. Essays
  I. Title

9 781735 236988

For Family and Friends who Stick Together

Works by Lee McQueen

Short Story Collection

Imaginarium

Poetry Collection

Things I Forgot to Tell You

Arusha: Poems & Essays

Novels

Kenzi

Celara Sun

Windrunner

The Cadis Evening

Screenplays

Kindred

SUDAN: The Lion of Truth

The Dark Fantastic: 12 Short Screenplays

I Disappear: 3 Short Screenplays

Non-Fiction

Writer in the Library! 41 Writers Reveal How They Use
Libraries to Develop Their Skill, Craft & Careers

Road Romance: Tales From the Book Tour

The Wind is an Eternal Searcher.

Because of its mobility, the Black Queen is the most powerful player in the game.

Table of Contents

Introduction

I wrote these works throughout a twenty-year span of my life from 2001 to 2021 and systematically registered them with the Library of Congress. Some aspects changed over the years while I fiddled with minor details. However, as I mull them over today, I find that the more some things change, the more most things really don't. I'm still who I used to be as a person... only MORE. And I find that I can still stand by what I wrote over twenty years ago!

I feel proud of my accomplishments and a sense of relief that I never held myself back to please anyone else. I didn't hide from life. I lived! No one caged me. I didn't allow it.

Instead, I allowed myself to be free to make mistakes (have adventures) and then learn the lessons that life taught me.

I'm so very thankful and grateful for every moment of clarity because, as is often said, knowledge is power. With knowledge, I've become stronger over the years. Wisdom and experience have high value. They are precious commodities that I would never trade away because I worked so very hard to earn them.

Writing songs based upon my poetry presented me with the similar excitement I felt when writing short screenplays based upon my short stories. Crossing genres from written to audio/visual helped me to discover so much more between the lines that I did not realize in the previous iteration.

Besides the technical aspects of form and function, I discovered the differences in pacing, intensity, and urgency. With songwriting, beat, tempo, rhythm, rhyme, chords, keys, so many aspects demanded extra attention. Outside my comfort zone, I relied upon several reference manuals to create... possibilities.

While I did record demos of these works to use as a guide, I am not a singer by profession. My default setting is **writer**, not performer. Therefore, I present to *you* the seeker, the speaker, the singer, the performer, these messages from the first half of my life. I wish you well in your interpretation.

Let it do what it do!

However, following a brief intermission, you'll definitely want to stay tuned for the second half.

Because the second half will be MORE.

Lee McQueen
14 September 2021

Why I Versify

[Reprinted from *Things I Forgot to Tell You*, 2nd ed [McQueen Press, 2007]

One weekend in April 2002, I reworked three poems I'd hidden away the previous year and sent them to a literary journal. The journal rejected "Bitter Woman, Solitude, and "Magic Night Special Morning, but the fact that I believed in them enough to submit them started the ball rolling.

That same weekend, I worked on three more poems combining two of them, "Universe and "God Gave This to Us," with elements from the Bible. The third, I developed from random notes I'd hidden away the previous year.

"Die a Little, See You See Me" (not included in this publication), "Dark Love Velvet Soul, Queen, Seven Months to Love You," and "Stuck on Maybe Not" quickly followed. So in one weekend, I finished nine poems. "M, When My Man Plays," and "Are You the Hero?" came to me a few days later.

From this point, the poems flowed like a river, mostly towards *Imaginarium's* short stories. "Bitter Woman" led to "Wild Hazy Beautiful Crazy" (and "M") which led to "The Confessions of the Dreamers." "The Confessions of the Dreamers" also features the poem, "Yellow Rain." I began to cross genres building stories around a few of the poems. A mermaid in "Waterscape" sings the "Universe poem to the wolf that she loves.

"Labyrinth of the Labor Realm" features "Painted," the poem. "God Gave This to Us," the poem, inspired the apocalyptic "A Day in the Life of ARES." Then I began hiding poems in the last blank page of various books. Maybe just to see if people would look further than the end.

What I like about poetry is the fact that it is interactive. The reader, and listener, if the poetry is spoken, meets the author halfway. One fills the poem with one's own reality and expectations. I described this phenomenon in "Painted." A lot like life and diamonds, poetry reflects an image back to you that depends on where you stand in relation to it.

Interestingly enough, while I prefer the written word, my strongest inspirations stem from song lyrics and spoken word. I almost always play music when I write. Paintings and film inspire me as well. Poetry has no boundary.

Lee McQueen
2 May 2006
rev. 23 March 2007

Lee McQueen, Red Velvet Cafe, Arusha, Tanzania, 2021

Air Electric, The © Lee McQueen

[mid-tempo dance, funk, rap]

[intro]

[chorus]
The air electric
Drop your side chick
Why don't you come and get
Everything you want, I let
The air electric
Drop your side chick
Why don't you come and get
Everything you want, I let

[verse 1]
Every inch of you
I know it over under through
Still more things that I can do
Honey, drive you koo-koo

[pre-chorus]
Sugar-frosted
Candy-coated
Mocha chocolate
Yeah, you know it

[chorus]
The air electric
Drop your side chick
Why don't you come and get
Everything you want, I let
The air electric
Drop your side chick
Why don't you come and get
Everything you want, I let

[verse 2]
They want what I got
I'm not afraid to shoot my shot
Lay it on super hot
Damn, you always hit the spot

[pre-chorus]
Sugar-frosted
Candy-coated
Mocha chocolate
Yeah, you know it

[chorus]
The air electric
Drop your side chick
Why don't you come and get
Everything you want, I let
The air electric
Drop that side bitch
Come home so I can fix
Where it hurts Imma lick

[verse 4]
Don't make me find you
I don't mind when you do
Wild things wild things do
Animals, that's right, us two

[bridge]
The air electric
The air electric
The air electric
The air electric
She don't even know how to hit it
(Boy, I do)
She don't got what I got to give it
(All for you)
How you ride second-class
(When you know I'm first)
And I know just how to quench
(That dirty, dirty thirst)
The air electric
The air electric
The air electric
The air electric

[pre-chorus]
Sugar-frosted
Candy-coated
Mocha chocolate
Yeah, you know it

[chorus]
The air electric
Drop your side chick
Why don't you come and get

Everything you want, I let
The air electric
Drop that side trick
Why don't you come and sit
On the saddle, tight fit

[verse 5]
Dirty dirty
Thirsty thirsty
Yeah, you be
Right back to me

[chorus]
The air electric
Drop that side chick
Why don't you come and get
Everything you want, I let
The air electric
Yeah we gonna wreck shit
Tied up in a twist
That's how much I really miss

[chorus]
The air electric
Drop your side chick
Why don't you come and get
Everything you want, I let
The air electric
Get real hectic
Boy, I come correct
This love's real legit

[chorus]
The air electric
The air electric
The air electric
The air electric
[outro]

Aloof Truth © Lee McQueen
[mid-tempo, pop]

[intro]

[verse 1]
Blue
The perfect jewel
A love so true
But friend of few
See through the rule
This glue holds two
So tattoo the mood
With Blue

[verse 2]
Violet
It's quiet and silent
Innocent
Might get to forget
That debt we kept
Just let it set
With no regret
For Violet

[chorus]
Don't lose me
Don't lose me
Don't lose me
Choose me

[verse 3]
Silver
Shiver and quiver
Now give her six rivers
Silk her off-kilter
Love her, live her
Forever
In Silver

[chorus]
Don't lose me (don't lose me, don't lose me)
Don't lose me (don't lose me, don't lose me)
Don't lose me (don't lose me, don't lose me)
Choose me

[bridge]
Behind the mirror's glimmer
Beneath the classy glass
Aloof space distance
Why, you ask
Faith to reach each
Stay connected
New direction
Affection not rejected

[verse 4]
Green
Dream the dream
See the scene
A clean stream and moonbeam

Seems so free
Just you and me
The perfect team
Ohhhh, Green

[chorus]
Don't lose me (don't lose me, don't lose me)
Don't lose me (don't lose me, don't lose me)
Don't lose me (don't lose me, don't lose me)
Choose me

[outro]

Bitter Woman © Lee McQueen
[spoken word]

She knows what's happening
It remains inside
There's nowhere to run
And there's nowhere to hide
The Church, her God
Wait to bring her home
Watch her damaged heart
Turn to black stone

Chemical love drug
Wrap her in a fog hug
Addict her mind
Clutch her snug

Fight the fear
Strap on the gear
They just jeer
Red light
Dead light
Bad fight
Rest tonight

Convictions are tight
Alone and lonely
Solitude every night
And the smile is phony
Chemical love
Beauty of life is clearer
But what do you see today?
Looking in the mirror
Dreary dark night

Bright brittle day
Send someone, Lord
Take this bitter away
Perfect morality
Everyone admires the view
But everyone also knows
The cold inside you
Search for an answer
Desperate to find
A way to reconcile
Broken glass in your mind

For everyone's approval
You give your life
The right thing to do
Don't cause such strife
Love him a lifetime
Tie your name to his
Lay down, have his children
Marital bliss?
"You stay. I go."
It's better this way
Don't tell the children
Let the children play

Empty space
Family disgrace
Lost race
Cracked face
Repair the breach
Try to teach
Lay a leech
Scream a speech

Chemical love
Smooth these rough edges
Disappear her from reality
Benson & Hedges
Where is love, Wild Hazy?
Will you ever know it?
Endless self-destruction
So you always blow it
View from afar
View from up here
What will happen?
When the emotions sear
How to learn from the past
When the past is still living
Southern-fried dysfunction
The gift that keeps giving
Who knows the future?
The future is not yet set
Hope exists maybe
If today will only let

Chautauqua Park © Lee McQueen
[spoken word]

I remember the scarlets, the crimsons, the magentas
purpled to violet and heliotrope
The yellows lemoned then saffroned to evening sun,
a lovely golden dream.
Little apricots and tangerines and peaches
wavered and shivered on the wind.
I breathed too.

Bed and blanket embraced me and
covered me and I hid so no one knew.

Crisp, crunchy, crumbly, snappy toys
tan and brown showered down upon me
chocolates and russets and chestnuts
cinnamons and hazels and gingers and fawns

And I felt so safe and so loved and
so happy and so home.

Even when the cold, icy beauty of
first white frost crept in overnight
the mirrors still reflected the sun and
melted down to silver swords or
broke into luminescent pearls and brilliant diamonds.

We were rich and did not know it.

Great fluffy mounds of cotton in which I rolled
an enormous expanse of marshmallows to eat all day
I made the angels fly and dance and sing feather-light.
My vanilla friends stood and waved to me row after row.

I still think of them sometimes, frozen,
surrounding me with a sparkly solid love,
an enduring devotion so many years ago.

Then green! Green! Green! Green!
Green made me feel so alive
Little emeralds sparkled and aquamarines shone.
Chartreuse so fully bright that it hurt me to look
I remembered to touch them.
And yet, I rejoiced because I knew that
this place was like no other.

I laughed and reached for the indigo and navy night
the azure and sapphire during the day.
Ever higher, deeply electric, livid and pure
Because life carried me on the wind.
I shivered and wavered from sheer delight.
It was always and never Chautauqua Park.

The circle clustered tightly and sheltered us.
Secret paths and secret places entranced us.
Lost, but not lonely, for hours
near the path, but not too close.
Rocks and stones
Sticks and branches
Brooks and nooks
Waited every day for
the runner
the jumper
the skipper
the hider
the seeker
Up and then down
around and

over and under
I did it all.
Reaching up beyond beauty to touch
the rest of the world
I can never go back.

Choose © Lee McQueen
[slow-tempo, pop]

[intro]

[verse 1]
Older now
Learning to forgive
Closer now
Wanting to live
Used to be
Something kind of strange
Somewhat crazy
And often pain

[chorus]
I don't want to lose
I want to win
I can always choose
When it begins

[verse 2]
Looking back
At misunderstandings
Life off-track
And love that can't be
Older now
Not that little kid
Show you proud
Things that I did

[chorus]
I don't want to lose
I want to win

I can always choose
When it begins

[bridge]
When will I be free
From the past that won't let me be?
How can I choose
To be free?

[verse 3]
Let it go
And wash it away
Moving slow
Dream of today
Breathe in deeply
Release the weight
Rock so gently
Shape your fate

[chorus]
I don't want to lose
I want to win
I can always choose
When it begins
I don't want to lose
I want to win
I can always choose
When it begins

[outro]

Damaged (But We Still Love You) © Lee McQueen

[spoken word]

When you gave us to them
For mirrors and beads and pieces of silver
You killed us both
Because we were always
Stronger together than apart
Some of you kept the
Generational wealth you earned
As slavers
Of different tribes
And to this day, you still
Make excuses
You smile and laugh
And you cannot understand
Why we do not laugh with you
You tell us to call you
Mama, Papa, Sister, Brother
But Mama, Papa, Sister, Brother
Would not do such things
Would not say such things
You call us guests
You call us tourists
And visitors and foreign
You call us strangers, even as you
Reach your hand into our pockets
We tell you what happened to us
After they took us
After they took everything from us
After they held guns and whips and knives
At our throats and dared us to

Speak our African language
Practice our African culture
Worship our African gods
Use our African names
Remember our African traditions
Remember our African ways

They promised a real death
Not just the living death of
A brainwashed zombie who
Performs for the master's delight
And delivers children for the master
To sell and build wealth for the master
The daily torture of the enslaved
The trauma and mental stress of
Constant hatred with no escape
The raped, abused, traumatized, tortured
Ones who managed to survive
And maintain some semblance of sanity
You look into their eyes
As they tell you their story
Of what happened after they took
Everything, including children
People that we loved and adored
People who made the living
Bearable
After they took everything we
Loved and believed in
You look, and you say
It's not so bad
You look, and you say
That was a long time ago
You look, and you say
You complain too much

You look, and you say
Work harder
Stop expecting
Stop talking
That language
We do not want to hear
Your words
Unless and until
You speak the way
That we will hear you

Speak our African language
Practice our African culture
Worship our African gods
Use our African names
Remember our African traditions
Remember our African ways

And forget
The four hundred years
It took you to develop a
New culture, tradition, history, religion
In order to survive
We tell you what happened to us yesterday
What happens to us today
What will happen to us tomorrow
The torture that remains
A part of our life every day
And still and still and still
You smile and laugh and say
Forget, forget all of that
Forget every last bit of that
Once more a brainwashing
Relinquish your identity once more

The four hundred years of your
Culture that you developed has
No place among us here
We do not accept the mutation
That you have now become
That they made you
Fix yourselves
Or else
Remain a stranger
In a strange land
A guest
A tourist
A visitor
A foreigner
An aberration
All we want from you
Is the wealth that you used
To relinquish to your master
That, we will accept
That and only that can belong to us
And then you may leave
The same way you came
As strangers

First Time © Lee McQueen
[slow-tempo, Sade-like torch]

[intro]

[verse 1]
Glow
Hide the shadow
Soft
Warm the night
Melt away the meaning
Candle's soft light

[instrumental chorus]

[verse 2]
Come
Take my breath
Please
Share yours with me
Cover my body
Together spirits free

[instrumental chorus]

[verse 3]
Love
Fill me slowly
Look watch my eyes
Tell me how much you care
Listen to me cry

[instrumental chorus]

[verse 4]
Wait
Feel my heartbeat
Touch
Feel yours too
Let me hold you tightly
Let me love you

[instrumental bridge]

[verse 5]
Glow
Hide the shadow
Soft
Warm the night
Melt away the meaning
Candle's soft light

[instrumental chorus]

[outro]

27   Lee McQueen

Gaslight (Yellow Rain) © Lee McQueen
[mid-tempo alternative soul]

[instrumental intro]

[spoken intro]
I didn't want to say it
But now I'm gonna say it
And you already know anyway
So go ahead and listen
Because you need to get this through your thick head

[verse 1]
Everything has reason
I always knew
Get a clue
No longer pleasin'
Introduce you to truth
Get your due

[chorus]
You lying ass liar
You're tired and fired!

[verse 2]
Trust in you
Things you say
Games you play
Only a fool
Tries to stay
Not walk away

[chorus]
You lying ass liar
You're tired and fired!

[spoken]
Oh yes!
We're gonna do this
Right now
In public!

[verse 3]
Used to hear
No yellow rain
Pissed in my face
Lies my dear
Bring the pain
Hell for my brain

[chorus]
You lying ass liar
You're tired and fired!

[bridge, spoken]
Please just stop with the games
You tired ass lying ass liar
You think you know
But you have no idea
Of who you're talking to
Are you serious?
Because no one believes you
You don't even believe you!
You are embarrassing yourself
And your entire family
And I'm laughing at you right now [laughter]

29   Lee McQueen

Because, at this point
You're ridiculous!
Is this the best you can do?
I deserve so much better than this
At least show some respect
And stop insulting my intelligence
And make some kind of effort
To keep your story straight, okay
I'm walking away
And now
You're talking to yourself
Like an idiot!

[verse 4]
Stories cannot last
When you smile at me
And gaslight me
While I laugh
Get a clue
No trust in you

[chorus]
And why should I?
You're a lying ass liar!
And you are tired and FIRED!

[spoken]
And I'm *still* laughing, okay
I'm going to laugh all day!
And probably tomorrow

[outro]

Get it from My Mama © Lee McQueen

[fast-tempo rap]

[intro]

Yeah! Yeah!
Yeah! Yeah! Yeah!

[verse 1]
Hair is black
Skin is brown
Built for distance
I get down
Yeah, I'm loud
Yeah, I cuss
Tell you off
I'm also soft but
(Only when time is right though)
Stay out my shadow though
Watching real close, so
Playing some games
Don't even know
I keep it tight, boy
Get to know me
Be surprised at
Things I be
Doing in the dark
Doing at night
Doing it right
Keeping it tight

[chorus]
Get it from my mama
Get it from my mama

Don't disrespect me
Yeah, you wanna

[verse 2]
Walking these streets
Keeping lights lit
Step to my man
Glad to see his d*ck
Gun in his pocket
Outerspace rocket
Make him see stars
All down to the socket
Got me shook
Got me shaken
Got me stirred
I don't be fakin'
Ain't fakin' nothin'
And he knows it
Get real wild
The way he glows it
Vibe real hard
The air electric
Everybody feel it, but
I'm his pick, so

[chorus]
Get it from my mama
Get it from my mama
Don't disrespect me
Boy, I'm gonna
Get it from my mama
Get it from my mama
Don't disrespect me
Yeah, you wanna

[verse 3]
Talk like street
When I first meet cha
Just an app
Not a feature
Low-key your ass
Under the radar
Don't see too fast
Don't get too far
Shine you on
Surveill you through
Night vision goggles (stalkin')
Do what I do
See what you're made of
See what's up
World don't love ya
Suck it up (buttercup)
Time to get tough
But I stay sexy
Hate the game
Don't hate me

[chorus]
Get it from my mama
Get it from my mama
Don't disrespect me
Boy, I'm gonna
Get it from my mama
Get it from my mama
Don't disrespect me
Yeah, you wanna

[bridge]
Where my giiiirls?
(Where they at?)
B*tch, we gotta talk!
('Bout this, but not that)
You look but you don't see (yeah)
You seek but you don't find (nah, you don't)
You think but you don't know (not a damn thing)
Cause I get it from my mamaaaa (yeaaaaaah)

[verse 4]
She military
She a crack shot
Twenty twenty vision
Southern hot
Hunter killer
She a slayer
What she made of
You can't play her (and you can't remake her)
She a church, a school, a college
Never raised a fool
She raised knowledge
Dollar out of fifteen cent
Ways out of no ways
Even when money's spent
Everyday's a birthday (heeeyyy!)
Rock the cradle
Entire generations
World is not enough
Make shit make sense

[chorus]
Get it from my mama
Get it from my mama

Don't disrespect me
Boy, I'm gonna
Get it from my mama
Get it from my mama
Don't disrespect me
Yeah, you wanna

[outro]

God Gave This to Us © Lee McQueen

[call and response, slow-tempo folk, gospel]

[intro]

[verse 1]
In the beginning, **God**
Created Heaven and **Earth**
In the ending, **Man**
Never understood their **worth**

[verse 2]
Gave us daylight
We seek to destroy
Gave us dark night
We fall into the void

[chorus]
God gave this to us
He left it in our trust
God gave this to us
He left it in our trust

[verse 3]
Land and water
So that we may have life
Trees and flowers
Cut down paradise

[chorus]
God gave this to us
He left it in our trust
God gave this to us
He left it in our trust

[verse 4]
Living creatures
To comfort and nourish
Trapped in cages
Struggle to flourish

[bridge]
God gave this to us!
He left it in our trust!
Why can't we just
Do what we must?

[verse 5]
Man in His own image
To care for the world
Greed and hatred
The evil unfurled

[verse 6]
Man killing Man
Because of a lie
God makes a way
So why can't we try?

[chorus]
God gave this to us
He left it in our trust
God gave this to us

He left it in our trust
God gave this to us
He left it in our trust
God gave this to us
He left it in our trust

[outro]

I Stand in Line © Lee McQueen
[fast-tempo pop]

[intro]

[pre-chorus]
Anyone out there?
Anyone who cares?
Reach to you only
Cold blank stare

[chorus]
Time?
What is time?
I stand in line
Important when it's yours
Don't care when it's mine
Time?
What is time?
I stand in line
Important when it's yours
Don't care when it's mine

[verse 1]
Sign this document
Fill out the form
Nobody cares
You were ever born
You're just a number
You're name don't exist
We're all AI
X off the list

[verse 2]
Yeah, our rules defy
Any understanding
Monotone always
Robotic demanding
I just work here
Put on the mask
Yes, I'm insincere
Don't even ask

[verse 3]
Guess what, I see you
Standing over there
Nevermind though
I really don't care
Don't talk to me
Don't even look
Best to call toll-free
'Cause your money's took

[pre-chorus]
Anyone out there?
Anyone who cares?
Reach to you only
Cold blank stare

[chorus]
Time?
What is time?
I stand in line
Important when it's yours
Don't care when it's mine

Time?
What is time?
I stand in line
Important when it's yours
Don't care when it's mine

[verse 4]
Voicemail's my friend
Now it's yours
Email, chat, or text
Humans divorced
Not like you're dying
Your life's turning to shit
Keep dialing while I'm smiling
Till your cold dead fingers quit

[verse 5]
It's not me it's you
It's not my department
Not my responsibility
Your problems make no sense
Is this your only id?
I don't have the time
Please excuse me
You're in the wrong line

[instrumental bridge]

[pre-chorus]
Anyone out there?
Anyone who cares?
Reach to you only
Cold blank stare

[chorus]
Time?
What is time?
I stand in line
Important when it's yours
Don't care when it's mine
Time?
What is time?
I stand in line
Important when it's yours
Don't care when it's mine

[verse 6]
Pay this fee
Pay this tax
My apology
We don't accept cash
No shirt no shoes
Well then, no service
No matter anyway
You have no insurance

[pre-chorus]
Anyone out there?
Anyone who cares?
Reach to you only
Cold blank stare

[chorus]
Time?
What is time?
I stand in line
Important when it's yours
Don't care when it's mine

Anyone out there?
Anyone who cares?
Reach to you only
Cold blank stare

[outro]

Lion Roars, The © Lee McQueen

[mid-tempo pop]

[intro]

[chorus]
The lion roars
I do not feel afraid
The lion roars
I never run away
I run to the lion
The lion roars

[verse 1]
I love to see him
This beautiful king's face
He rides like the wind
He always wins the race
I run to the lion

[verse 2]
Eyes shine like jewels
Teeth that gleam white
Every time he sees me
He always smiles so wide
I'm in love with the lion

[chorus]
The lion roars
I do not feel afraid
The lion roars
I never run away
I run to the lion
The lion roars

[verse 3]
He draws me near
Every time he roars
I laugh with the lion
To the sun beyond we soar
Together with the lion

[bridge]
Closer and closer to
The lion
Eaten alive by
The lion
Devoured by
The lion
I'm captured
By the lion
Forever with
The lion
The lion

[verse 4]
Ohhhh, and I'm happy now
With the lion
Together forever
With the lion
The lion roars

[chorus]
The lion roars
I do not feel afraid
Ohhhh, the lion roars
And I never run away
I run to the lion
The lion roars

[outro]

On Street K © Lee McQueen

[spoken word]

In my dreams I visited that place
I saw and walked away
Nightmare and vision of K Street
I saw and walked away

A little boy leads me to the door
I look back on it today
Turns and points and grins to show
That everything's okay

Drug dealers, pimps, and their customers
Argue over the pay
Half-naked hookers scream obscenities
I heard and chose to stay

The place police no longer police
Once the sun goes away
The man at the door is surprised at me
His face turns completely gray

He gestures at me whispering, "Just leave
And for your life pray!"
The package I borrowed, I set it down
The boy waves me away

So down the stairs I'm lucky for my life
But I'm late for Society Soirée
And what should I do, a stranger there?
My journey is home and holiday

For his disobedience, for forgetting the rule
On the window ledge he lays
The boy, that boy who helped me there
Screams, "I didn't betray!"

They hold him by his feet... for a while
Because I saw and so did they
The next window up high, a punishment
A little girl's skin they flay

I saw it. I heard it.
And yet, I walked away
I valued my life. I wanted to live.
And so, I walked away.

The neighborhood stopped, frozen, shocked
And watched the entire little play
On this street in filmed slow motion
Voyeur's Lunatic Matinee

The third window up high another child up there
This is the price that they pay
The price for doing things... unasked
They are examples to display

To the next street and the next block
I stumbled far, far away
Keeping straight remaining neutral
Saving only my own life, to my dismay

Who am I? Who are you?
I'm just... trying to convey
I saw it all. I saw all of it.
I admit that I was there that day.

No siren no whistle
Just me walking away
I am them. They are me.
But I walked away

Court to cell it happens to us
Behind these bars, here to stay
They all shout. They try me.
But I never look away

Outside my cell now I walk towards the yard
Two hours of sun today
My accusers grip my wrists hard
Against the steel and say

"You saw our children. You did nothing.
You go the exact same way.
The children are gone and now so are you
You see Death come today."

I went to that place that godless place
I saw and I walked away
But it's over now. I no longer dream
Of what I saw on Street K

Painted © Lee McQueen
[slow-tempo, pop]

[intro]

[verse 1]
Awaken
Awaken and see an empty room
The sun, the sky, the tree, the air, the Earth, the moon
Locked inside
Locked inside sexy silver glass
Cannot hide
Cannot hide just break me don't ask
The Hated

[verse 2]
Make it
Make it all ready to face that way
Little paper cuts and spitted poison today
Perfect diction
Phony fiction of regular reality
Shake the hand
Smile so wide then devour all of me
The Hated

[verse 3]
Jaded
Jaded 'cause you said it with no proof
Do you ever see what I see ever, do you?
The other side
The other side you hide away from me
Diamond filter
Killer glitter distorted reality
You painted

[verse 4]
Naked
Fake it no money shield for you
The lock, the bar, the gate, the wall, the gun real soon
And you lied
You lied just like you lied in the past
So much pride
So much pride grasping and crass
The Hated

[chorus]
Yeah, I'm gonna make it
Gonna make it, make it
I'm gonna, gonna make it, make it
Watch me, watch me, watch me
Watch me make it
Yeah, I'm gonna make it

[outro]

People Live, The © Lee McQueen

[spoken word]

The death-bringer fails
The people live
Everything you take
The world will give

Stronger than you
Evil disappears
Happier than you
Despite your sneers

What made this beast
So wicked, so monstrous
A pathetic loser
That no one could trust

We know the darkness
Hidden under the smile
The simple inch we gave
You turned into a mile

Not fit for humans
The animals won't have you
Repulsive to all
Can't walk down an avenue

The lair you tricked out
Is now your prison cell
Your hollow corpse
Alien indwelt

You are not one of us
We all know it
The people live
The alien doesn't

Phantasmic Fantastic Fantasy © Lee McQueen
[mid-tempo alternative rap, funk, ode to Prince]

[intro]

[verse 1]
Happy now, I fly
I glide and then I slide
Sparkled electric
All glitterfied
Inside outside
I decide to ride
Cause Oz is always
Bonfa fide good time

[verse 2]
Unmasked, I pass
Thru the Looking Glass
Orgasmic elastic
Atlantis splash
Mind tripped, squeezed
And dizzied free
Relaxed Neverland and
Melted mystery

[chorus]
Phantasmic fantastic
Fantasy has to be
So real, a thrilly thrill
Surreal reality

[verse 3]
Wonderland aquarium deep
Blue-green speaks to me

Floating flash patterns
Falling to the sea
Spiritual adventure
To Narnia I picture
Haze of time in Heaven
Cause God's a little richer

[chorus]
Phantasmic fantastic
Fantasy has to be
So real, a thrilly thrill
Surreal reality

[bridge, 1st key change]
Spearmint peppermint
Hyacinth labyrinth
Starfish jellyfish
Sunkissed odalisque
Moonlit chocolate
Magnet orbit
Incense pretense
Friendship endless

[chorus, return to original key]
Phantasmic fantastic
Fantasy has to be
So real, a thrilly thrill
Surreal reality

[verse 4, 2nd key change]
Swim through shades of color
Hold hands with a lover
Time now to discover
Everybody my brother

Rocket to the sun
Pretty papillon
Wave a magic wand
For Lilliput and beyond

[chorus, return to original key]
Phantasmic fantastic
Fantasy has to be
So real, a thrilly thrill
Surreal reality
Phantasmic fantastic
Fantasy has to be
So real, a thrilly thrill
Surreal reality

[outro]

Reverie
[slow-tempo folk]

[intro]

[verse 1]
Reverie
Day dreams of pinks and greens
Reverie
While I'm lost in thought
And revelry

[instrumental chorus]

[verse 2]
Reverie
Of blue on blue silver
Reverie
And trees, and flowers, and springs
All of these things

[instrumental chorus]

[verse 3]
Everywhere, what I see
The windmills and water towers
Reverie
While I walk by
My heart sings

[instrumental chorus]

[bridge]
Everyday is beautiful

Everyday is wonderful
Everyday I'm thankful
Everyday I'm joyful
I'm singing everyday
And I'm so grateful
For a life that's full

[verse 4]
Misty rain
Wind and white clouds race me
Reverie
And I always try to win
Reverie

[instrumental chorus]

[verse 5]
Not asleep
As the sun rises and sets
Every moment I get
I'm dreaming wide awake
Singing while I walk

Reverie
Reverie
Reverie

[outro]

Seven Months to Love You © Lee McQueen
[mid-tempo, pop]

[intro]

[verse 1]
I knew at our first meeting
Happy at the coffee shop
To hear the man's reading
You captured my heart
September through November
Chill floats in the air
Still in cold December
I'm warmed by your stare

[chorus]
Try to walk away
But I never get too far
Try to turn away
But there you always are
There's no mistake
You're already in my heart
Fantasies of you
Dreams that won't come true
Imagining it's you

[verse 2]
New Year and new days come
Bring forth the adventure
Embarrassed to find someone
Smiling at your picture

We laugh and run around
February's only a game
Can't keep my heart underground
Cause you smile my name

[chorus]
Try to walk away
But I never get too far
Try to turn away
But there you always are
There's no mistake
You're already in my heart
Fantasies of you
Dreams that won't come true
Imagining it's you

[bridge spoken]
I inhale you when I breathe
I feel you on my skin
So to hide I must leave
My heart to defend
I care so very deeply
Wanted us to be friends
But the smile and warmth make me
Vulnerable again

[bridge sung]
Seven months to love you
Five months to leave you
So hard to walk away
Maybe next lifetime
We will be together

[verse 3]
They say that our eyes
Are windows to our souls
March and spring surprise
Feelings still uknown
Good-bye to you, my brother
One-way love has to end
I know that you love her
April Heart will one day mend

[chorus]
Try to walk away
But I never get too far
Try to turn away
But there you always are
There's no mistake
You're already in my heart
Fantasies of you
Dreams that won't come true
Imagining it's you

[spoken]
Seven months to love you
Five months to leave you
So hard to walk away

[sung]
Maybe next lifetime
We will be together

[outro]

Silk and Silver © Lee McQueen
[fast-tempo rap]

[intro]

[verse 1]
Yeah, I adored you in silk and silver
Leather black, and how you delivered
The words you said
The way they slithered
How I shook
How I shivered
The way you made
Me always quiver

[chorus]
When will I see you again? (baby)
When is the next time?
Why do you make me wait? (baby)
Waiting is a crime
When will I see you again? (baby)
When is the next time?
Why do you make me wait? (baby)
Waiting is a crime

[verse 2]
Yeah, I miss you man, I adore
That's why I always come back for more
The way you move
The way I soar
How I glow
How you roar
And my skin still thirsts
For silk and silver

[chorus]
When will I see you again? (baby)
When is the next time?
Why do you make me wait? (baby)
Waiting is a crime
When will I see you again? (baby)
When is the next time?
Why do you make me wait? (baby)
Waiting is a crime

[verse 3]
I love this man
Love him hard
The way he wants it
High regard
How good I get it
That's how I give it
All the time for silk and silver
Every time for silk and silver

[bridge]
Look, you know the deal (yeah)
Man, you know how I feel (yeah)
And you know where I be (yeah)
Let's do it ('cause you want it too, yeah)
Today, right now (ohh)

[verse 4]
I adore you in silk and silver (you know it)
Leather black, and how you deliver (on it)
The words you say (say it)
The way they slither (ooh)
How I shake (ahh)
How I shiver (ooh)

The way you make
Me always quiver (yeah)

[chorus]
When will I see you again? (baby)
When is the next time?
Why do you make me wait? (baby)
Waiting is a crime
When will I see you again? (baby)
When is the next time?
Why do you make me wait? (baby)
Waiting is a crime

That's how much I want you (baby)
Silk and silver (do it!)
Let it do what it do ('cause you want it too)
I got all the time for silk and silver!

[outro]

Solitude © Lee McQueen
[spoken word]

Away from the crowd and the loud
I have a chance to feel and think how
Thoughts of what life should be
And remember what life is actually

I can let down my guard
Dance, play, love, and live extra hard
Break the silence with my own laughter
Read a book chapter by chapter

No arguments or interruptions
Naked soul without corruption
I can feel silly, sad, mad, and glad
Remeber the best times I've ever had

Visit the park and breathe clean air
Let rain hit my face and wash through my hair
Ride my bike far and fast
See how long my endurance lasts

Listen to Prince, Lenny, and Sade
Lay around in bed all the long alone day
Watch my favorite movies again and again
Think of funny messages and jokes to send

Should I break this quiet spell?
Find people with stories to tell?
Or wait a little longer maybe
Too much kind of smothers me

Pink sky turning orange for dawn
See cold dew on the lawn
Let the sun warm on my face
I should give up this rat race

Casting thoughts to dreams and fears
Mocking myself with little sneers
No longer important because God is here
And when I need Him, He remains near

I love you, Lord, all by myself
I exhale, relax, put problems on a shelf
Thank you, Lord, for loving me
Alone with You is where I like to be

Stuck on Maybe Not © Lee McQueen
[mid-tempo, pop]

[intro]

[chorus]
We have yesterday, Baby
Stuck on maybe not
But who's to say, Maybe
'Cause I never forgot

[verse 1]
Remember that time
When we were so young
Crazy and excited
All breathless from the fun

[verse 2]
Love those college years
Partied and danced
Sometimes went to class
Flirted and romanced

[verse 3]
You were so crazy
I was so cool
I always delighted
To let you play the fool

[pre-chorus]
And we let it slip away
Still wonder where you are today

[chorus]
We have yesterday, Baby
Stuck on maybe not
But who's to say, Maybe
"Cause I never forgot

[verse 4]
Left me and then
Wandered off to war
Life got real serious
And my heart tore

[verse 5]
Unbelievable phone call
"Marry me," you said
Never the right time
So, "I love you instead."

[instrumental bridge]

[pre-chorus]
And we let it slip away
Still wonder where you are today

[chorus]
We have yesterday, Baby
Stuck on maybe not
But who's to say, Maybe
'Cause I never forgot

[verse 6]
Last time together
Intense new emotions
No resolution
And no magic potions

[pre-chorus]
And we let it slip away
Still wonder where you are today

[chorus]
We have yesterday, Baby
Stuck on maybe not
But who's to say, Maybe
'Cause I never forgot

We have yesterday, Baby
Stuck on maybe not
But who's to say, Maybe
'Cause I never forgot

[outro]

Sun Shines, The © Lee McQueen

[spoken word]

How can I describe the blaze?
How can I show the glow?
How can you understand the heat?
Our life, our health, our strength
The joy that God's greatest gift brings

Yes, we, who love You
Your children that You raise
We lift our hands up
We dance and play and revel
With the greatest gift that God brings

Because you endure
Before us, with us, and after us
How wonderful you make the world
And we have life everlasting
Because of God's greatest gift we sing

Highly wanted, highly desired
Endurance of a thousand ages
We need you to always stay with us

The sun shines so bright
White, yellow, orange
Tangerine, peach dreams
To chase away the cold of winter night
Life, the greatest gift God brings

Tragedy's Dancer © Lee McQueen
[uptempo, pop, rock]

[intro]

[verse 1]
One they crushed
And destroyed
Power lust
The little toy
Not one chance
The circumstance
Too afraid

[verse 2]
Whatever you feel it's real
What happened to you?
Soul they steal and still
Spirit subdued
Lost out there
No one to care
Drift away

[chorus]
Who are you now?
Where did you go?
Scream out loud
Don't listen anymore

[bridge]
Even though you joke and play
You cry sometimes
So unreal, you never say
About that time
Who are you now?

[verse 3]
Be my baby again
If I grieve
Are you still my friend?
If I leave?
Tragedy's dancer
Tell me the answer
I want you to say

[chorus]
Who are you now?
Where did you go?
Scream out loud
Don't listen any more

Who are you now?
Where did you go?
Don't look away

[outro]

Universe © Lee McQueen
[mid-tempo folk, gospel]

[intro]

[verse 1]
Generations live and die
Yellow turns to gray
Sun rises in the sky
Moon takes sun away

[verse 2]
Light returns to shadow
Fire burns to smoke
Jaundice ends in pallor
Wind blows south and north

[chorus]
The way of the world
We remember we forget
Universe is circular
Give what you get

[verse 3]
Wood weathers dark
Dandelion goes to seed
River runs to the ocean
What was shall ever be

[verse 4]
Eyes to see forever
Ears that don't listen
Gold will be silver
The endless lesson

[chorus]
The way of the world
We remember we forget
Universe is circular
Give what you get

[spoken bridge]
We were given even the whole world
But the world was not enough
But there's still time
To make things right
Let the people say

[sung bridge]*
Amen
Amen
Amen
Amen
Amen

[verse 5]
Universe is circular
You become what you hate
Future will be history
You remember it too late

[chorus]
The way of the world
We remember we forget
Universe is circular
Give what you get

Amen (hallelujah)
Amen (hallelujah)
Amen
Amen
Amen

[outro]

*Traditional gospel, public domain.

When My Man Plays © Lee McQueen
[mid-tempo jazz, in the spirit of Chaka Khan]

[instrumental intro]

[chorus]
When my man plays
Passionate grace
Like just a taste
When my man plays

[verse 1]
Music I hear
Sounds like my dear
Like to be near
Music I hear

[instrumental break]

[chorus]
When my man plays
Passionate grace
Like just a taste
When my man plays

[verse 2]
Play on soldier
Play it bolder
Take me over
Play on soldier

[bridge]
And when he plays I get bolder
Yeah he plays it like a soldier

Like a soldier
I get bolder
So take me over now
Take me over now
Let me hear it now
'Cause I feel it now
Play it soldier
Play it soldier
Play it soldier
Play it soldier

[instrumental break]

[chorus]
When my man plays
Passionate grace
Like just a taste
When my man plays
When my man plays
Passionate grace
Like just a taste
When my man plays

[instrumental fade]

Wild Hazy, Beautiful Crazy © Lee McQueen
[fast-tempo, alternative rap]

[intro]

[verse 1]
Wild Hazy
Stormed into my life
Brassy sassy racy spacey
Frenzied pepper spice
Brilliantly flashed
She flamed with no shame
Clashed and then smashed
And then claimed the pain
You left when the storm
The torrent that formed
Came and hurricaned your dreams away

[sung pre-chorus]
Don't hide from what you are
Because you are the same

[spoken chorus]
Don't tell me all about life
'Cause life is just a game
I said, don't tell me all about life
'Cause life is just a game

[verse 2]
Beautiful Crazy
She surprised them all
Shocked and rocked but stopped
Right before the fall
Cruel... so angry to defend

Scorched... but now she's free
Driven by the wind again
And gripped a piercing breeze
She soared and seared
And danced, such grace
Loved but truly feared, debased and erased

[sung pre-chorus]
Don't hide from what you are
Because you are the same

[spoken chorus]
Don't tell me all about life
'Cause life is just a game
I said, don't tell me all about life
'Cause life is just a game

[verse 3]
Pretty Lady
Floating the carousel
That cool attitude
In this rough world
Chemical miracle
Gives you the best in dreams
Still, in spite of it all
You shine, you sheen
Take me where you are
Far away from here
Far away from me, I long for the serene.

[bridge, call and response]
Why does it have to be this way?
(I don't make the rules)
I don't want to live that way
(I don't want to lose)
Some days I want to run away
(From this hard knock school)
Life is just a game to play
(But I'm not a fool)

[verse 4]
Definitely Maybe
Just cannot handle you, Baby
You stay just to say
But you want to play free
You know what they see
What they think when they asleep
For you only you
They allow you to peek
Fighting a system that
Kidnaps your name
Don't hide from what you are
Because you are the same

[sung pre-chorus]
Don't hide from what you are
Because you are the same

[spoken chorus]
Don't tell me all about life
'Cause life is not a game
I said, don't tell me all about life
'Cause life is not a game
Don't tell me all about life

'Cause life is not a game
I said, don't tell me all about life
'Cause life is not a game
'Cause life is not a game
'Cause life is not a game

[outro]

Wind is an Eternal Searcher, The © Lee McQueen
[slow-tempo, pop]

[intro]

[verse 1]
Chasing your shadow
Watching the wind blow
Wanting our love to grow
But I never, ever did know
One day we were happy
Birthdays kind of sappy
Up in your arms you'd wrap me
I loved you then, Daddy

[chorus]
Searching the wind
For the hero
You keep saying you're my friend
You're the hero

[verse 2]
Heavy sounds of silence
Should have caught the loud hints
Took a while to convince
Rarely seen your face since
Empty house of horror
Looked for you tomorrow
Filled so full of sorrow
Have any love I can borrow

[chorus]
Searching the wind
For the hero

You keep saying you're my friend
You're the hero

[verse 3]
Visits just a token
With the babysitter moping
Family circle broken
Attorneys all have spoken
Yes, you are God's best friend
Church loves you to no end
Abandonment you can't defend
Such a tired, typical trend

[bridge]
Are you the hero?
Are you the man who said good-bye?
Left though I cried and tried
To make everything all right
Are you the hero?
Or was it all some simple lie
I no longer ask you why
Are you hero?

[verse 4]
Don't really need you
Don't care if I never see you
Would never want to be you
'Cause nothing could ever please you

[chorus]
Searching the wind
For the hero
You keep saying you're my friend
That you're the hero

Don't tell me anymore about a hero
When it's zero, zero, zero
You're not the hero, hero, hero

[outro]

Audio Book Track List

1. Title :08
2. Copyright 4:21
3. Dedication :06
4. Works by Lee McQueen :48
5. Quotations :11
6. Table of Contents 1:33
7. Introduction 2:54
8. Why I Versify 2:58
9. Air Electric, The 2:52
10. Aloof Truth 3:19
11. Bitter Woman 2:22
12. Chautauqua Park 3:04
13. Choose 4:01
14. Damaged 4:12
15. First Time 1:39
16. Gaslight (Yellow Rain) 2:47
17. Get It From My Mama 2:38
18. God Gave This to Us 2:50
19. I Stand in Line 4:01
20. Lion Roars, The 3:08
21. On Street K 3:40
22. Painted 2:41
23. People Live, The :55
24. Phantasmic Fantastic Fantasy 2:46
25. Reverie 2:26
26. Seven Months to Love You 4:15
27. Silk and Silver 1:31
28. Solitude 1:49
29. Stuck on Maybe Not 2:19
30. Sun Shines, The 1:07
31. Tragedy's Dancer 2:46
32. Universe 2:27

Print Edition, E-book, Audio Book, and Audio CDs available via many online retailers.

Visit the official McQueen Press website: *http://mcqueenpress.wordpress.com*

Audio CD Track List

Eternal Searcher Song Book volume 1, spoken
1. Introduction 2:54
2. Why I Versify 2:58
3. Bitter Woman 2:22
4. Chautauqua Park 3:04
5. Damaged 4:12
6. On Street K 3:40
7. People Live, The :55
8. Solitude 1:49
9. Sun Shines, The 1:07
10. About the Author :32
11. Author's Note 3:16
12. Acknowledgments :32

Total run time: 27:32

Eternal Searcher Song Book volume 2, A-P
13. Air Electric, The 2:52
14. Aloof Truth 3:19
15. Choose 4:01
16. First Time 1:39
17. Gaslight (Yellow Rain) 2:47
18. Get It From My Mama 2:38
19. God Gave This to Us 2:50
20. I Stand in Line 4:01
21. Lion Roars, The 3:08
22. Painted 2:41

Total run time: 29:33

Eternal Searcher Song Book volume 3, P-W

23. Phantasmic Fantastic Fantasy 2:46
24. Reverie 2:26
25. Seven Months to Love You 4:16
26. Silk and Silver 1:31
27. Stuck on Maybe Not 2:19
28. Tragedy's Dancer 2:48
29. Universe 2:27
30. When My Man Plays 2:19
31. Wild Hazy, Beautiful Crazy 2:54
32. Wind is an Eternal Searcher, The 2:54

Total run time: 27:07

Print Edition, E-book, Audio Book, and Audio CDs available via many online retailers.

Visit the official McQueen Press website: http://mcqueenpress.wordpress.com

About the Author

Lee McQueen enjoys writing, research, water colors, gardening, and traveling. She has been a librarian, a bookstore owner, and a substitute teacher and holds an MLS from SUNY-Buffalo, a BA from Xavier University, and coursework in public affairs at the University of Texas at Austin. Now editor and publisher at McQueen Press, her projects include novels, poetry, songwriting, short stories, screenplays, and greeting cards.

Author's Note

Air Electric, The
You have not, because you ask not. But you gotta give to get. That's all.

Aloof Truth
A cool exterior hides sensitivity and fear.

Bitter Woman
Even when you don't want to know, sometimes, you know.

Chautauqua Park
It is the most beautiful place and time... on the surface.

Choose
After years of waiting, one kind word smooths away the abrasions.

Damaged
This is a complicated conversation about survival.

First Time
Things happen when you share breath, soul, spirit.

Gaslight (Yellow Rain)
"Every shut eye ain't sleep." Some wise someone said that once.

Get it From My Mama
I am so proud of this woman.

God Gave This to Us
If God knew then what He knows now, would He have ever created Man?

I Stand in Line
A person's life falls apart. A bureaucrat services the bureaucracy rather than humanity.

Lion Roars, The
Its... not really about a lion...

On Street K
An ode to Edgar Allen Poe.

Painted
Sometimes you shrug it off. Sometimes you don't.

People Live, The
The mind of a sociopath is a deep black hole of evil.

Phantasmic Fantastic Fantasy
After three *mojitos* on the shores of a Cuban beach resort, there's no such thing as pain.

Reverie
Walking around enjoying the gifts of love and life in the sun and air.

Seven Months to Love You
They call it puppy love.

Solitude
It's really nice to get away from it all sometimes.

Silk and Silver
Not puppy love.

Stuck on Maybe Not
They said "no." But they didn't say "never."

Sun Shines, The
The greatest gift ever given? Life.

Tragedy's Dancer
The most useless emotion must be guilt. It helps no one.

Universe
Everyone knows it always comes back around. Those who don't know, should wait just a little longer.

When My Man Plays
He played with his eyes closed. Passion and emotion stirred the air. He destroyed the room. Then calmly surveyed the chaos.

Wild Hazy, Beautiful Crazy
People play the hand they're dealt.

Wind is an Eternal Searcher, The
Hypocrisy sucks.

Acknowledgments

Thank you to the honorable former president of Tanzania, John Pombe Magufuli. You saved many lives, including mine. You provided sanctuary.

You left a legacy of honor as a man of high elevation, well-deserving of worldwide respect. Well done good and faithful servant to the nation of Tanzania and the world.

I will never forget you.

Arusha: Poems & Essays
2021
2nd Edition, E-Book version
ISBN 978-1-7352369-4-0

Available via many online retailers.

Visit the official McQueen Press website:
http://mcqueenpress.wordpress.com

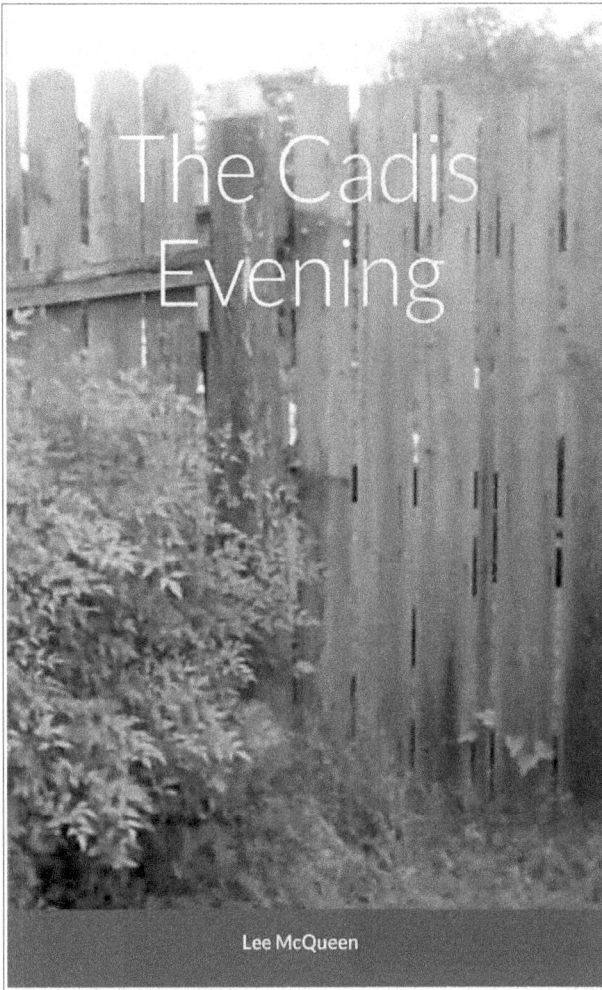

The Cadis Evening
2020 [2016]
2nd Edition, E-Book version
ISBN 13 978-1-7352369-5-7

Available via many online retailers.

Visit the official McQueen Press website:
http://mcqueenpress.wordpress.com

I Disappear: 3 Short Screenplays
2020
E-Book version
ISBN 978-1-7352369-0-2

Available via many online retailers.

Visit the official McQueen Press website:
http://mcqueenpress.wordpress.com